HE'S LYING SIS

Uncover the Truth Behind...
His Words and Actions

VOLUME I

STEPHAN LABOSSIERE
@stephanspeaks

He's Lying Sis – *Uncover the Truth Behind His Words & Actions, Volume I*

Editor & Creative Consultant: C. Nzingha Smith

Formatting: Ya Ya Ya Creative – www.yayayacreative.com

ISBN No. 978-0-9980189-3-5

Table of Contents

Introduction

*W*hen did dating become so difficult? Every day I get flooded with emails, direct messages, comments on my social media accounts, and I have coaching calls with women who are operating in a state of chaos, confusion, and unhappiness. A huge source of their frustration is from what's become frequently awful dating experiences. As well as unfulfilling, yet lingering, "it's complicated," situationships.

Many women would argue that using the word difficult to describe dating is putting it way too mildly. So many women have or are experiencing dating frustration and relationship disappointments, they're swapping more war stories than boasting about happily-ever-after success. The nonsense is so common, it might make you think that there aren't any good men out there. You might feel discouraged and want to give up hope regarding your ability to experience a great relationship in this lifetime.

Loss of hope, turns into you settling or entertaining situations you don't belong in. Hence my use of "situationships" vs. "relationships" to describe your possible current scenario. Being discouraged can cause you to become blinded to the red flags you may recognize in a potential mate. You might be afraid to address the red flags because you feel like, "Well, can I find anything better? Why leave this guy, who's a jerk, for an unknown jerk? He may be my best option. Let me figure out how to deal with him and make it work."

Even worse, you might be thinking, "Better to have a piece of a man than no man at all," depending on your situation. These types of thought processes and justifications regarding dating and relationships are wrong. However, I understand that this type of thinking is exactly what's going on in the minds of many women nowadays. Not understanding how to navigate through the treacherous waters of the dating landscape is a struggle for most women. This is the main reason why I wrote this book.

I'm seeing too much damage. This type of rationale is helping to create or continue the negative cycles of relationships that begin based off mixed signals, lies, and confusion. Dating with these dynamics in place means you're dealing with a man you don't need to be dealing with in the first place. It can be a struggle trying not to get caught up in the nonsense that some men will try to throw your way.

However, let me make something very clear before I go any further. I'm not here to bash men. I believe and can tell you with all certainty that there are great men out there. Wonderful men still do exist in this world. Men you will be attracted to. Men who can love you the way that you desire. Men you can build an amazing relationship with. Men who are capable of being your Boaz and the man God has for you.

However, if you can't get past the wrong ones, you'll never reach the right one. Many times, even if you get to the right one, you're likely to be so worn down and damaged from all the crap you already went through, you won't know how to receive him properly. You won't know how to embrace him, and you won't trust or allow yourself to love him.

I don't want this to be the case for you. This book is meant to help bring awareness to the potential damage that comes from chronically dating the wrong guys. I want to help you break free from the negativity and cynical thinking. I don't want you to miss him or the opportunity to experience a healthy and fulfilling relationship. I want you to be able to recognize the games and lies so you can avoid them entirely.

I don't think you understand how detrimental it can be to get caught up in what seems like a harmless situation at first. However, when it turns into one, two, five years of your precious life and your being dragged along in a relationship with a man who is not meant for you, it's extremely harmful and no good will come of it.

I don't want this to continue to be the norm for you or anyone else.

I'm writing this book because I feel it's important that I do my part to help protect you. I want to keep you safe. I want you to experience and receive the relationship that is right for you. I want you to be able to experience the quality of life you deserve. I want you to be happy. Free from the nonsense. Free from the headaches. Free from the stress that situationships can bring.

Again, I am not writing this book to bash men. I'm writing this book to create a clear distinction between acceptable and unacceptable behavior in dating and relationships from a male perspective. I want to steer you clear of the wrong men. I am here to pour love, clarity, and encouragement into you so that you can stay on the right track and get what is truly best for you.

My hope is that by writing this and its companion books, I'll help you, save yourself from a lot of dysfunction, unnecessary tears, and unhappiness. I want to prevent the countless nights of venting to friends, family, and anyone else who's willing to listen, about your frustrations with your dating life and situationships.

I'm hoping you'll embrace the information and insight in this book. I hope you will allow it to confirm what you might already sense in your gut. I hope it will encourage you to accept the truth and act, if needed, in your situation.

Be careful not to jump to conclusions while reading and just decide that the man you're currently dealing with is lying about everything he's ever said to you. Jumping to conclusions and being reactive are not the right way to use the information I'm sharing with you. This book is not meant to create chaos or confusion.

The question mark on the cover indicates that you've possibly already been having doubts about things or don't know how to distinguish between what is true and what isn't. I'm going to lay out the information you need. I'm going to give you an understanding, so you'll know how to decipher when he is indeed lying, or at the very least, see if you need to dig deeper to gain clarity on a situation.

I want you to continue reading with an open mind. Please resist the urge to pick up or carry a negative perception of men and dating from what I will share with you throughout the book. Again, I'm writing this book for you to use as a healthy resource on your road to find the right relationships for you.

Focus instead on the good results that will come from this newfound knowledge once you apply it in your life. I want you to be filled with positivity, hope, and optimism as you read. I want you to get excited about the fact that by reading this book you're positioning yourself closer to the real thing. After reading this book you'll be able to save precious time navigating the dating waters because you'll know how to clear out the nonsense, making a way clear for the right person to enter your life.

Even though I'm a man of God, I didn't write this book from a spiritual angle. I'm speaking from a more practical perspective because these are the issues that I'm constantly helping women work through and get clarity about. However, like everything I share with you, there needs to be a balance. This being the case, I will always encourage you to pray about what someone tells you, myself included.

Pray about the information presented to you and make sure you're getting divine guidance on the practical matters of life. I don't want you to take the information in the wrong way and run with it in the wrong direction.

I want you to fully understand how each scenario might help you make better decisions while dating and in your relationships. Some of things I share may apply to you. Some may not. You might not be reading this book for you now, but the information I share, might need to be passed on to someone you care about, a friend, family member, or co-worker.

Again, I will always encourage you to pray about everything before you act on anything. I want you to be divinely guided to do what's best for you and your specific situation at the proper time.

It's equally important that you trust your intuition dealing with the information that I will share. Your intuition is a blessing. It's there to lead, guide, and protect you. It's not something you should ignore. It's something you should trust.

A lot of what I'm going to share with you in this book isn't going to be new to you. It may not be a huge revelation because deep inside you knew it already or at least sensed it before. My words will simply serve to remind or confirm what you already felt within you. Hence the importance of listening and trusting your intuition.

Moving forward, I want you to begin to trust your intuition more. Learn how to listen and follow it because you can save yourself from situations you don't belong in, before they even start. You'll also be able to tune into and embrace the relationships that you do belong in. It's a win-win.

Trusting in your intuition will be more reliable than trusting your eyes. Let me be clear here, sometimes where you belong isn't going to look like or line up exactly with the ideal picture you have in your head. Sometimes what can turn out a complete blessing in the end, may not make any sense in the beginning. Therefore, you need to learn to rely more on your intuition.

God wants to lead and guide you as to where you need to go and who you need in your life, but you must be able to hear Him, trust, and obey His guidance. Your intuition is God's voice speaking to your spirit.

Take a deep breath. Mentally prepare for what I'm about to share with you. Again, some of what I share, might sound familiar and come in agreement with what you already knew. However, some of what I share might be a real gut punch or a hard pill for you to swallow.

Always remember, I'm sharing this insight with you from a place of love. I'm telling you these things with the hope that I can now start to repair relationships and help you improve your love life. At the end of the day, I want to see everyone happy and fulfilled in love. I want you to find your true peace, your true happiness, and your right relationship. Okay, now I think we're finally ready to begin.

Let's go.

He Says,
"He Doesn't Want a Girlfriend, but Acts Like Your Boyfriend"

*M*eet Cindy. Cindy came to me for help with getting clarity on the actions of a guy she was dating named Eric. She was confused by too many mixed signals.

When Cindy met Eric, she really liked and clicked with him easily. They started dating and things were going well. After a few of months of spending quality time and getting to know Eric, she felt she could see herself in a relationship with him. Naturally, Cindy wanted to know if they were progressing and if Eric felt the same way about her and the potential between them. Since it had been a few months, Cindy felt it was fair to probe and see if he was ready to formally couple up.

However, whenever the topic of a relationship or titles came up, Eric always danced around the subject. He refused to give her any straight answers. His replies included, "Oh, I'm too busy. I need time. Let's just go with the flow." Since Cindy really liked Eric and things seemed to be going well, she decided she didn't want to rock the boat. She accepted his replies and went with the flow.

Time goes on. Eric is still not pushing for a relationship, but he's doing everything that a boyfriend would do.

When Cindy and Eric were together, they were hugged up in front of friends, they were always going out, spending nights together, and doing everything a couple does. Eric even bought her a gift for her birthday and gifts on other gift-giving holidays and special occasions.

As a result, Cindy felt like she was in a relationship with Eric, but he still wasn't officially calling it a relationship. Cindy was beyond confused. She honestly didn't know what was going on or what the big deal was about him making them official.

Cindy "went with the flow" for over a year. The entire time, Cindy was left unsure about Eric and his desire for her in his life, which caused her a lot of anxiety and planted the seeds of insecurity, causing her to question herself on every level. When she finally reached out to me for help, this was her mindset:

"It seems like he really likes me, but he doesn't want to have an official relationship. I don't want to let him or the "non-relationship" go because it feels good. I want companionship. He's doing enough to make me feel like, maybe I should just give this some more time and see what happens."

After a couple conversations, Cindy did admit that there were times where she realized, Eric wasn't the guy that she needed him to be, or the fact that he didn't really behave like he was a committed guy in a relationship.

Shortly after our initial conversation, Cindy found out Eric was talking to another woman. Next thing you know, he wasn't just talking to this other woman casually, he was with her. He entered a relationship with this other woman and backed away from Cindy completely.

Cindy was hurt to the core, distraught, and further confused by everything. She swore off men and immediately put her walls up. The experience created a lot of negative energy within her that we had to work together to get her through.

She honestly didn't understand what had happened all in the blink of an eye. How could Eric do this to her? They were pretty much like boyfriend and girlfriend and had been operating that way for over a year. Why would he not cement a relationship with her, but then turn around and be so quick to get into a relationship with this other woman?

Cindy's scenario is the perfect illustration of the danger of entertaining a man "who doesn't want a girlfriend but acts like your boyfriend."

What exactly does that mean? What is really going on here?

Let me make it plain. When a guy is engaging in *boyfriend* behavior with you but doesn't want to initiate a relationship of any kind or give it any titles, it's because he doesn't want to be committed to you. That's the bottom line here.

When you're just kicking it, no matter how many boyfriend activities he engages in, no matter how much he talks to you, no matter what you're able to get out of him in that situation, the fact remains that if there's not an *official* title given, he is free to do as he pleases. He is not obligated to you.

When a man is in an official relationship, he knows there's a higher level of commitment and obligation required. A serious, committed relationship is something that he must approach with a more mature and a more genuine attitude.

When you're just the woman he's kicking it with—let's say one day you're sick. You call him to ask him to go get you some medicine at the store, he knows he doesn't have to if he doesn't want to. In his mind, he's not obligated to you. He can choose to do it or not. Don't get me wrong, he might still do it out of the kindness of his heart, but he always has the freedom to say no. He always has the freedom to entertain other people. He always has the freedom to fall short if he feels like it because he's not your boyfriend or in a relationship with you. —he's not committed to you in any way.

You might be thinking, "Well, why all the boyfriend behavior? Why all the hugging and kissing and bringing me around friends, even bringing me around his family? Why is he doing all this if he doesn't want a relationship?"

Simple. He enjoys the relationship benefits you're giving him. Just like you, he enjoys the intimacy. He enjoys the companionship. He enjoys all that you're bringing to the table. Even with all of that, he also knows he doesn't want to be obligated and committed to you.

I understand that this might be a bit harsh. However, I'm not saying this to hurt your feelings. I'm sharing this with you to help you avoid the BS. He could really like you. He could even view you as a great woman and still not see you as the woman for him.

I admit that it's a very tricky thing. It trips up a lot of women. He's going to give you a lot of the energy that says, "I like you. I even value you to a certain extent." As true as this is, it doesn't mean he sees you as the woman he really wants to be coupled up with. It also doesn't mean he sees you as his future wife.

Unfortunately, a lot of men out of selfishness, greed, narcissism in some situations, are still going to try to get what they can get out of you. Even though they're not prepared to give you what you're looking for, which is most often a commitment.

They'll validate their non-committed behavior by saying, "But I'm still doing all these nice things. I'm still treating you well. So why are you having an issue with this?"

An official relationship brings you one of the most important things you need as a woman, security. Until a man gives you security, you're always going to feel unsettled. In non-official relationship situations, it almost always becomes toxic because, at some point, this is going to bother you. Being unsure will make you feel restless. This is going to rack your nerves and drive you insane.

The longer you stay in this type of situation, the harder it is to pull yourself out it because you have time invested that you will want to see a return on. You'll rationalize and analyze the situation to death and come up with a million reasons why you should stay in it.

However, now that you know what it is, if you're currently in any kind of non-relationship, even if you're deep in it, I need you to immediately recognize why you must let it go and not continue to give the situationship your time. Abort the mission ASAP. If you're not in this situation, good. I don't want you to get into a situation like this at all. You're now able to recognize it right away. I want you to avoid it altogether.

You might be asking yourself, "But didn't Stephan just say the guy actually does have feelings for me? If he's behaving like my boyfriend, could it be he's just not ready for a commitment right now? If the feelings are there, maybe I should hold on and see what happens?"

No, you shouldn't hold on and see what happens. Let's get technical here. Okay, yes, he has feelings for you. Who cares? They're not strong enough for him to want to commit to you. If he's not willing to commit to you, you don't need to hold on to false hope that the non-relationship will turn into anything more.

This is the point I want to drive home here. It's not that he doesn't enjoy you. It's not that he doesn't view you in high regard to some extent. It's not that he doesn't think you'll make a great partner.

It's the fact that he knows you're not the one for him. You know what else? It's perfectly okay because he's not the one for you either.

Deep within, you know he's not the one for you, but you've been rationalizing past it, trying to hold on to the little things he does here and there that matter to you. You've allowed yourself to look over the red flags, to push past your doubt and your intuition saying, "He's not it. I don't belong with him."

Listen to yourself. Follow through on your own inner guidance.

Another question you may have in this type of situation is, "Will he eventually want a relationship with me? Could he change his mind about his feelings for me?"

It's highly unlikely. If he doesn't see you as a woman, he wants to commit to in the first year, six months, whatever the time frame, he probably won't magically decide to change his position. He won't suddenly believe you're the woman for him and want to be with you in a relationship.

Now, I'm not going to say it's impossible. I'm not going to say it's never happened. I'm saying it's highly unlikely. Therefore, it's not the approach you should take. However, I believe in balance, so let me also shed light on the fact that some men can and do change their minds about where they want a woman to fit in their lives.

Let's say he does come to a place where he entertains having a relationship with you. Sometimes a man will change his mind and embrace a relationship after not being willing at first. However, I firmly believe in this situation, he's still not serious about being with you long term. He may have just come to the conclusion, "Okay. Let me just go along with her desire for a relationship to pacify and shut her up about it. I don't want to lose the benefits she provides. I can give her something fake for now." I'm using the word fake here because he's going to give you a fake relationship to appease you so he can keep getting what he wants/needs from you.

If you're asking yourself, "How do I know if it's a fake relationship?"

The biggest indication of a fake relationship is if you're giving him everything he needs and he's not giving you what you need, but he's still willing to take what you're willing to give him. If this is the case, it's a fake relationship.

Real relationships aren't one-sided. So, if he's taking, taking, taking, it's fake. Even if in the beginning, he was doing all this nice stuff, it's very difficult for most men, not all, there's always exceptions to the rule, but for most men to maintain that behavior consistently if they're not serious about you. At some point, you're going to see the situationship become lopsided. It's going to be more about what you give him rather than what he's willing to give you.

Ask yourself a question. "Does he take my feelings seriously?" If a man is always dismissing your feelings, making excuses, and deflecting, it's a fake relationship. Him not taking your feelings seriously, means he's not serious enough about you.

I've seen tons of situations where any time the woman would bring her concerns to the guy, he would just turn the tables on her. "Oh, you're tripping. You're always complaining. Why aren't you ever happy?"

However, they don't acknowledge the fact that they're not doing much to make their woman happy. However, he'll deflect in the moment to simply take the spotlight off himself and not have to take any responsibility for his part in the situation.

Pay attention to what happens when you try to express yourself and feelings to him. If he's unwilling to embrace how you feel, it's not a real relationship.

On the other hand, I've seen scenarios where the newly interested guy finally agrees to a relationship with the woman, but it ends up being nothing more than a consolation prize. He might think, "Well, I'm ready to settle down now. She's been here. Let me go ahead and make her the one."

You might be thinking, "Well, that's not so bad. At least I get what I want too and he's finally embracing what's in front of him, me."

Wrong. Whenever a guy settles on being with you, when he figures he owes it to you or you're just the best option available at that moment, you're headed for a disastrous relationship. That's not what you want. That's not what you need. Happiness and fulfillment are not going to be found in that type of relationship because the whole relationship is predicated on what you're doing for him. He's not going to have the motivation necessary to be the man you need him to be, consistently.

The reason he's in the relationship won't be because he's in love with you. It's not because he realized you're his soul mate or that he has this amazing connection with you. It's a rationalization. He simply said, "Oh, she's the best available right now. Let me just go ahead and get with her since I'm ready to settle down." Chances are, he's more likely to eventually cheat because again, you're not what he really wanted.

Let me reaffirm my point here. Don't stick around in these situations waiting for this guy to finally pick you. Listen to me, no one needs years to see if they have a connection with someone. It doesn't take us years to tell if a person is someone, we can really see ourselves with long-term. Yes, there may be some exceptions to the rule, as always, but for the most part, people decide very quickly, especially men— believe it or not—whether they can see true relationship potential within the first few dates.

One thing you should understand about a lot of men is that sometimes even just by looking at you, they've already compartmentalized where they're going to put you in their life.

Upon meeting you, exchanging a few conversations, and having a few interactions, they'll say to themselves, "This is a woman I'm going to just sleep with. This is a woman I might entertain a relationship with. This is a woman I would consider wifey material and could see myself marrying."

Many times, if not always, a man has already figured out pretty quickly the role that he wants you to play in his life. He's already decided where you stand. Most men are quick to make these decisions, which means changing their mind is nearly impossible or if it does happen, it's going to take a very long time.

Yes, there are some things that happen in the flow of time and sometimes there might be the case of him not realizing how you fit in his life immediately. It might take him longer to see the potential. However, in most cases, he sees, decides quickly, and that decision sticks. If he doesn't see it quickly, it's probably because there wasn't a strong connection present in the first place.

Bottom line. When he's acting like your boyfriend, but he's telling you he doesn't want a girlfriend, stop acting like his girlfriend.

Stop engaging and giving him the benefits of having a girlfriend. Stop rewarding him if he's unwilling to give you the security you need. To be honest with you, the real security is marriage, not merely a relationship.

However, I understand that marriage is not everyone's top priority. Everyone's not trying to get married tomorrow. We live in a society that engages in boyfriend and girlfriend relationships as adults. Okay, fine. At the very least, he should be able to give you a committed relationship.

Let's be real. If he can't even attempt to give you that, why are you continuously giving him what he desires? Stop making it so easy for him. Stop being so convenient for him. Stop allowing him to make withdrawals without demanding that he makes deposits back into you. Mature relationships are all about reciprocity. He will do what you allow him to do. Going forward, if you've entertained this before, don't allow it to continue.

Be honest with yourself. You've been talking long enough. He knows who you are. You've spent quality time. Either he wants to be with you, or he doesn't. If he's not ready for a relationship, if he claims he just wants to go with the flow, let him know, "Cool. You flow that way and I'll be flowing in the opposite direction."

Don't be fooled by boyfriend behavior initially. A man who is serious about you, a man who really wants to be with you, won't just be content with acting like your boyfriend. He will make sure he makes things official and takes you off the market. He will want to ensure that you're all his, leaving no room for chance or him losing you.

He Says, "He's Too Busy for a Relationship"

*M*eet Alicia. Alicia started dating Michael, a very successful entrepreneur. When they met, Michael worked long hours, putting a lot of time into his business success. Alicia on the other hand worked in the healthcare field. Her job was structured with set hours and she enjoyed having more stability in her life.

Despite their different lifestyles, Alicia and Michael hit it off right away. However, Alicia noticed quickly after they met that if she wanted to hear from Michael, she had to be the one to initiate the communication. She was the one reaching out most of the time. Even when she did reach out, sending Michael a "good morning" text, it might take him three or four hours before he responded. Calling him was even more complicated because he often couldn't talk and would take forever to return her call.

Alicia felt there was a lack of attention and a lack of interest on Michael's part as a result. This started to bother her, but you know, Alicia really liked Michael and when they did talk it was great conversation. They had a lot in common and she really felt like it was worth her trying to deal with. Even though she didn't like it, she put up with it, and they continued to date.

Time goes on and nothing changed. Eventually, Alicia felt the need to say something to Michael about the issue. She brought the issue to his attention:

"Michael, I feel like you aren't giving me enough of your time." Alicia mentioned to him as calmly as she could one night during dinner.

"Alicia, I really like you from what I've experienced so far. I really want to see this go somewhere, but at the same time, I'm a really busy guy and I just don't have the time that you need from me right now." Michael replied.

Alicia chewed on her food and Michael's word without saying anything else about it. She believed Michael, but she knew she had to make a decision. Did she want to continue forward and see how the relationship would progress? or Was she going to move on and not be bothered with dealing with the lack of time and Michael's busy schedule, which he claimed was the reason behind his not reaching out.

A scenario like this is easily clarified. He has time, just not for you.

In Michael and Alicia's situation, I'm not going to discount the fact that he genuinely liked Alicia and was making some level of effort. However, the reality in most situations when the guy says, "I'm just too busy," it really means, "I don't want to put in that kind of effort for you." It also means, he doesn't view you as a high enough priority in his life to take time away from what he considers to be a higher priority.

In Michael's case, his business and work were a higher priority than Alicia and she wasn't important enough (yet) for him to justify taking time away from it to give to her. However, reasons can vary. It could be his children, family issues, social commitments he had before he met you. A variety of things could be going on here and there are many reasons why he may not make time for you.

At the end of the day, the man determines what he's willing to make time for. If he's not making time for you, there's a problem. Now initially, while he's getting to know you, he might ration his time because he's not sure you're worth it yet. However, after spending time with you, he must make the decision to now prioritize time for you if he's really interested.

Understand that there may be an inability, initially, to give you his time and attention. He'll need a window to transition out of always being about work to now making time for someone he wants in his life. This can be very difficult for a lot of people. It might take time for him to adjust and learn how to fit the new relationship into his current life schedule.

However, if you've given him an adequate amount of time to figure it out, expressed your desire to spend more time with him, and he makes no effort to change his schedule, it's a huge red flag you shouldn't ignore. If he continues to pacify you with excuses, you'll need to allow that to carry more weight than your attraction to him or you're interest in a relationship.

Think about it. I'm sure there have been times where people wanted your time and you've used the "I'm too busy excuse," but you weren't that busy, you just didn't want to be bothered with them, or you didn't want to give your time to them. Plain and simple. You must be honest with yourself and recognize when he simply doesn't value you enough or does not value the potential of the relationship enough for him to sacrifice and make time for you or it.

Now, I also want you to be mindful of when you might be unreasonable with your time request. What do I mean by this? Well, I've seen a lot of situations where the woman is just not satisfied, even though the man is doing his best and making time for her. They're hanging out often and getting a lot of good quality time in, but the woman simply wants more.

A lot of times this happens when a person doesn't have much else going on in their life. I'm not trying to be insulting in any way here. When you have more time on your hands than the other person, you could be more demanding on the other person without knowing it. Due to having a lot more time on your hands, you desire or require more time from your partner simply because you're bored. Your request for more time has to do with you trying to fill up your day. You want more of their attention because you're not doing anything else.

I want you to think about this for a second. If you find yourself in this situation right now, consider your position as well as his. Be aware of when this is the case and not the fact that he isn't giving you adequate time. When your need for more time is not really a need, but a desire because you have nothing else going on, this isn't fair to him. You're creating an issue where no issue really exists. Even though it might be difficult for you to admit, it's necessary. If you're in this situation, you need to pull back and figure out what's missing in your life and what you need to do about it.

A relationship is meant to enhance and add to what you already have going on. You're never supposed to make a relationship or a man your entire world. It's very important for you to create proper balance in your life. Having proper balance will mean you won't need to pull so much from your relationship or require so much from your man. Doing so causes friction and issues in the relationship that can and should be avoided.

Be honest with yourself and him about what you really need. It's one thing to say, "I need to hear from you daily." It's another thing to say, "We need to talk on the phone for four hours every single day." Do you really need to be on the phone with him for four hours a day just to feel like he's into you? Is that necessary? Many working adults won't be able to live up to those type of expectations. People are juggling a lot in their lives daily. So, you'll need to look in the mirror and ask yourself are you being reasonable with your requests. You'll also need to figure out where your needs are coming from. Are they from a healthy or unhealthy place and adjust them accordingly.

Understand that it's not someone else's responsibility to entertain you all day because you don't have anything else better to do. It's not fair to them. A desire to get to know someone is healthy. Looking for someone to occupy your time because you don't have much else going on, is not. If you don't have a lot going on, find other things that you're interested in doing and start doing them. Doing so will enrich your life and create a balance within the relationship. Taking this approach will allow you to still enjoy your partner without putting an unnecessary strain on the relationship.

Okay, so let's talk about when being too busy is the truth and not just an excuse or sign of disinterest on his part. Now, I still stand by the case I made previously that most times when a man says "I'm too busy" it's an excuse. I'm a firm believer that people make time for what they want to make time for. Essentially, they make time for the things that are important to them. I think plenty of people have made that comment or have stated that quote and it's very true.

However, I do believe if you're dealing with an entrepreneur or a very driven, goal-oriented, ambitious man, he will genuinely have a difficult time understanding how to create balance in his life when it comes to work and the new relationship. His inability to make time in the beginning is not evidence of him not being serious about you. It doesn't mean he doesn't really like you or that he's not interested in being with you. He just doesn't know how to do it because he's become a slave to his work.

Understand that he has lived his life like this for an extended amount of time. So, when someone comes along, even that somebody he's really feeling and really into, he still won't honestly know how to make the shift. He won't know how to create the balance and make it all work.

The theory of being in a relationship and being in one is completely different. Many people want to be in a relationship and can't wait to meet that special someone. However, they're not practicing relationship habits while single to help them get prepared for it. They have no idea how to create balance between their current conflicting priorities. Let alone how to add something much more valuable on top of everything they have going on and make it all work. This issue has happened among both men and women. So, even though I'm talking about men here, it's just as important for you to begin to practice making time for what you want to create in your life.

Don't wait until you find a relationship to create time for a relationship. It's always risky to try to learn everything on the job. What do I mean by this? Well, if you're single and you usually work late into the night, you can start giving yourself a cut-off time so that you know how to do it when the relationship comes, and it won't be so difficult. During the window of time you now have free, you can spend time doing some personal development activities that will help you in areas you'll need when you enter a relationship. Again, make time now so that it's already a habit.

Juggling too much is a dangerous game. You end up losing out when you don't figure out how to make space ahead of time. Hoping someone will just magically fit into your life and be convenient sets you and the potential relationship up for failure. You're hoping for the other person to just fit, so that you're allowed to hold onto all the work and other things that you've already been doing. Theoretically, it makes sense, but it's not practical. It's also not a good course of action to take if you meet someone who you're really into.

Take a moment to evaluate your own life right now. If you're a busy woman, ask yourself, "have I created time for a man and relationship in my life?"

Yes, this book is about what men do and how they behave, but always be willing to look in the mirror and ask the tough questions. Are you creating time for a relationship in your life? Do you have the balance that you need for a healthy relationship? You may be the busy one in some cases. Not learning how to balance everything out in advance will cause you to miss out.

Back to the men. The fact that he's busy can be true. Lack of time isn't always used as an excuse. It doesn't always imply malicious intent, lack of interest, or lack of value for you. It's honestly just human nature. We all try to make things work for us as conveniently as possible without a lot of disruption. Again, he might just need a little more time to figure out and understand how to create that balance in order to make room for you.

Now, that doesn't mean you stay with him and deal with it. I'm simply explaining the different scenarios that might come out of this situation to bring clarity. However, he still needs to understand that if he wants you in his life, then making time for you is necessary, period. There's no way around it. He's going to have to learn.

Now if you want to give him some suggestions on how to achieve balance and make it work, great. If you want to point him in the right direction, cool. That would be awesome. However, don't continue to seriously date him or get into a relationship with him until he makes the time adjustment and begins to prioritize you in his life. If you do, you're essentially enabling his struggle. You're enabling his lack of focus or awareness on how to give his work and give you proper time and attention. He's got to get that together one way or another. It's not wise for you to proceed forward with him until he does.

My suggestion to you, if you're facing this situation, is to simply explain to him your position like Alicia did with Michael. She didn't respond to him right away. However, after she thought it over, was honest with herself about her needs, and prayed, she brought the issue back up to Michael on a latter occasion. After she had had enough and it seemed like there was no light at the end of the tunnel, she decided to express her feelings to Michael and let him know where she stood.

"Michael I'm seriously interested in you. I want to see where this can go. If you're serious too, I need you to figure out how you can make time for me and work. If you're not willing or ready to do that right now, then we can't continue forward. We can't date or progress into a relationship. If you're not prepared or able to make the necessary time adjustments, then I'll need to move on. When/if you get to the point in your life where you can and are willing to do so, feel free to reach out and we can take it from there."

You don't ever want to give a man permission to continue behavior you don't like. By doing so, you are essentially saying to him, it's acceptable to you. Be honest with yourself. Are you going to be happy with him never having or making time for you on a regular basis? If you're genuinely okay with his lack of time for you, then continue forward. However, if you know it bothers you, if you know it makes you unhappy and could open the door to you entertaining other people, it needs to be addressed and corrected. If not, the relationship or dating needs to end.

If you want to continue forward and exercise patience dealing with his busy schedule, try to work towards a compromise. A compromise is finding a middle ground that both sides can be happy with. Once you two agree on a middle ground, if you're still not happy, there is a good chance you didn't really compromise, you sacrificed. Sacrifice means you gave up something that's essential to you and your happiness for the sake of the other person. I'm not saying sacrifices never work in a relationship. However, it all depends on how long you've been together. If you begin the relationship sacrificing things that are essential to you, it's very likely you'll be unhappy for the duration of the relationship.

One of the biggest mistake's women make when dating is not being honest about what they need or want to see from the man in the dating process. If you're the type of woman who genuinely loves to get a "good morning" text, let that be known in the beginning. You need to let him know exactly what you need so he can decide whether he can meet your needs and expectations. This way, you'll know right away if he is willing to step up to the plate and give you exactly what you're looking for. If he can't, then there's no point in continuing and dragging it out.

Let me point out here that Alicia didn't give Michael an ultimatum. She clearly expressed her feelings and let him know where she stood. He understood her position. However, he didn't have a solution to the situation at the time. He also liked her and didn't want to make the situation worse, causing Alicia to become disinterested in him completely. He agreed to part ways in hopes that they'd have a chance to try again once he figured out how to fit her into his life.

Michael didn't come to me for coaching. However, I have worked with countless men, like Michael, who have come to me for advice regarding help on balancing a newly found love interest and the rest of the priorities in their lives.

I usually simply recommend that they try asking the woman what she wants. Only she can tell him how much communication she needs from him daily/weekly to feel satisfied while trying to build a relationship. Once she communicates that she'd like a call at least two to three times a week and that would be enough to start. He then needs to decide if he can meet that need because now, he's clear about what she needs from him. Boom, problem solved.

Too many times, women want the man to figure it out. When it comes to a busy man, who's already pressed for time, figuring it out complicates what could be simple. Tell him and he can do it or decide it's something he's not willing to do. Taking this approach saves both of you from headaches and wasted time. Once a man has clarity on what is required of him and what your needs and desires are in the relationship or in the building of a relationship, when he's into you, he has no problems making it happen. However, many times women aren't clear about what they want and need.

Please don't come to me with the argument, "Why do I have to tell him, he should know. It should be common sense."

Listen, common sense isn't always common. The reality is that you don't know what he's been exposed to before you. Don't make assumptions about him automatically knowing what you as a woman will like or need. Relationships aren't one size fits all. Sharing what you like and what you don't, helps him make you happy. It helps him get to know you. It helps him feel more secure about doing things for you because he doesn't have to guess or figure you out. He wants to be successful if he's pursuing a relationship with you. He also wants to know that giving you his time is a good use of it and that you won't waste it or abuse it. It's unfair to him if you aren't giving him any direction to begin with.

Remember that communication is a big piece of the successful relationship puzzle. Always be willing to talk about things upfront, from the beginning. Always be willing to let him know how you feel. This will keep the confusion, misunderstandings, and arguments to a minimum.

Even though Michael didn't know how to proceed at the time in moving forward with Alicia, he did what she requested and reached out once he figured out and practiced making time for the relationship. He realized after they stopped communicating that she was important to him and he too wanted to see if they could progress into something serious.

The second time around, Michael was more attentive to Alicia. He initiated more of their telephone and text communication. He also made sure she felt his desire and interest in her. He was vocal about his feelings and he did his best to back them up with his actions. So, even though it didn't work out the first time. The fact that Alicia communicated clearly gave Michael the confidence to try again and to really do the work to make it work with her. His being busy was not as important after all when it came to someone he was interested in and wanted to get to know.

Again, I still stand by the statement that people make time for what's important to them. However, don't jump to conclusions and dismiss a man before seeking clarity in the situation. Being too busy could be the truth and he might struggle with figuring out how to make time for you. Being too busy is not always an indication of him not being serious, that he's lying, or that he's making excuses.

Communicate clearly to see where he really stands in this type of situation. You now know how to handle the different scenarios and if you pray and seek clarity, you will also know what your best course of action is for each situation moving forward.

He Says,
"He Loves You,
but He Doesn't Show It"

Meet Michelle and Robert. From the time they started dating, Robert was very open and expressive to her about his feelings. He didn't seem to hold anything back. Even revealing that he felt he loved her after only a short time into them dating.

Michelle wasn't used to being with a man who was so free about sharing his feelings and emotions. The change of pace was refreshing, and she welcomed it with open arms. However, Michelle also noticed that Robert never really seemed to back up his words with consistent actions. He wasn't very considerate of her when they weren't together. There were always long delays between texts. Sometimes he would go stretches without reaching out to her and she would end up having to call or text or not hear from him at all. She didn't feel like she was a priority in his life. When she expressed her concerns, he never took ownership, he just deflected, and distracted her from the issues by telling her that he loved her.

Michelle was often battling confusion as to whether Robert was sincere in his feelings. His verbal expressiveness and willingness to say, "I love you and want you in my life," wasn't really backed up with any action. However, the fact that he shared his feelings at all, often allowed his words to overshadow his lack of showing Michelle his love outwardly. Michelle felt like, "Okay, there's something here worth holding on to. I should definitely keep moving forward with him."

Eventually Michelle and Robert entered a committed relationship. However, the whole time she felt like there was something missing. A void of some kind. Robert was terribly inconsistent. His actions didn't match up with the love he was constantly professing. Robert had more excuses than he had anything else. More times than not, he would forget little things. He also wasn't as affectionate as she liked. One day, Michelle decided to ask him about it.

"Robert, you claim you love me, but you don't show it. Sure, words are nice to hear and I'm thankful that you feel comfortable sharing your feelings for me. However, I also need you to act like you love me. Why don't you ever show me by doing things for me that speak louder than words?"

Robert claimed, "I just have a hard time showing love. The family I grew up with wasn't very affectionate. They didn't show love to each other. Love wasn't ever expressed outside of words. It was kind of a given. When it was said that was enough. It's uncomfortable for me to be affectionate and show my love with actions."

Michelle was immediately sympathetic and felt sorry for him. She felt like, "Okay, I just need to be understanding and patient with him. At least he's telling me he loves me. He must clearly love me. I'm going to stick it out, hoping he will begin trying to find ways to show me his love as well."

To that I said, "Hell no." Hell no to keeping it going. Hell, no to believing you need to hold on to this situation because he's saying the right things. Even if he's telling you he loves you, if he's not backing it up with action that's a problem.

Ask yourself, "Why would a man be so willing to say he loves me, but not also be willing to show it? Aren't men usually more able to show their love over expressing themselves verbally and saying they love you?"

Exactly. Typically, men struggle more with expressing their love and feelings verbally. They often get tripped up when trying to figure out how to say all the sweet things a woman wants to hear. This is true more times than not because men are usually not raised to be communicators. It can be a struggle for a man to open up and truly embrace his feelings for you, let alone tell you all the time that he loves you. Of course, that doesn't apply to every man.

Let's consider for a second that Robert is telling Michelle the truth here. He might really struggle with expressing his love with actions. As I just pointed out, men typically struggle more with verbally expressing emotions and feelings. However, in this scenario we're talking about a man who can say he loves you, but who doesn't show it. At the end of the day, if he can say the words, and he means them, there should be no reason why he can't show his love to you.

Let's use the example of intimacy. I'm not talking about sex here. Sex is a form of intimacy, but it's not the only form. Plenty of men will have no problem having sex with you whether they have feelings for you or not. However, if they're not really feeling you, they'll have an issue being intimate with you in other ways. They'll struggle with showing you affection, whether it be in public or in private. Other forms of intimacy include, hugging, holding hands, caressing you, kissing you, listening to you, being thoughtful and considerate towards you. These all constitute forms of intimacy that require real feelings from a man for him to do them without your needing to ask him.

Now it's possible that the man you're dealing with is someone who didn't grow up in an environment where outward expressions of love were given. He might not have had the experience of being in a family that hugged each other or kissed. Now as an adult, it's hard for him to behave in a way that he's not used to. If that is truly his issue, then it's simple, he's not ready to be in a relationship.

I have no problem acknowledging that some men legitimately struggle in certain areas with expressing their love. I have no problem giving a man in this situation the benefit of the doubt. That being said, if he claims that this is his issue, I still don't think you should remain in the situationship with him. I don't think it's a strong enough reason why you should be patiently waiting on him to magically overcome this issue. If he's unable to give you what you need and desire, it's not fair to you to stay in the situation waiting for him to figure it out or not.

As adults, we're all able to learn the things we need to learn in order to function successfully in life and in love. We need to collectively get out of using our "dysfunctional childhoods" as an excuse for why we grow up to be dysfunctional and mistreat people we claim to love and care about. I'll get more into that in the next book, Finding Love After Heartbreak, Volume I.

Even if you feel you love him, your love won't be enough. A successful relationship requires more than love alone. Love is more than a word or a three-word sentence. Love is also more than someone's random actions towards you. Love is in our spirit. It's who we are. It's a part of our very being.

A man who's really into you, who cares about you and wants to be with you, is not going to be satisfied with just expressing his love for you in words. He's going to want to show you how he feels about you as often as he can. He'll have the internal need within himself to show you he loves you with actions as well as his words.

Understand that love is about giving. Love is not just taking, taking, taking. No, honestly, love is giving, giving, giving. If you're dealing with a man who is proclaiming to love you, but he doesn't give of himself for you, he does not love you. If he doesn't pour into you, then he's lying when he says he loves you.

If you're in this situation, it's important to take a step back and evaluate whether his words and actions are lining up. Don't let his sweet words blind you and cause you to overlook the clear red flags that are telling you something's not right. If he can't show his love for you in his actions and learn how to speak your love language, there's no point in continuing forward with him.

Let's say that you have sympathy for his reason that he's uncomfortable showing his love for you.

He confides in you that he honestly has an issue and is generally clueless or uncomfortable with showing his feelings. Okay, cool. You now need to ask him the question, "What are you going to do about it?"

Just because he has an issue in this area, it's still not acceptable for him to continue this way. He should be willing to do something about it if he really does love you and is serious about the relationship progressing. He might need to go to counseling. He might need you to communicate the ways you need to feel loved and you all might need to create a structure to where he's able to practice acting out his feelings. Whatever it takes, he must be willing to take steps to correct the issue and do something about it.

Depending on whether or not he's willing to correct the issue, I would say to you, "Be patient with him. Work with him because he's willing to now put in the effort." If it's the latter and he just wants you to feel sorry for him and uses his issue as an excuse, justifying that's just the way he is. I would say to you, "Save yourself and walk away." If he continues making excuses, shoots down your suggestions, or simply tries to validate his behavior, your next step needs to be to move on. Period.

Again, if he's not willing to do anything about his own issues, why should you care more than he does and stay? It's not going to work. There's no point in beating a dead horse. He's not even willing to try to do his part and improve himself.

Let me illustrate this point further and show you how ridiculous it is to accept his excuses for not wanting to work on himself. Let's say you want to hear from him more often. Let's say you feel like he doesn't call you enough. You want to feel like he's thinking about you and that he's considering you when you all are not together. Calling you is the way he can show you that. It would make you happier and bring the two of you closer together in your relationship. It's a win-win.

You say to him, "Baby, listen, I want to hear from you more often. I wish you would call me at least twice daily."

He responds to your very sensible request by saying, "Listen, I think I call you enough already. I only feel comfortable calling you once a day. I don't know what you want me to do. I don't get how we're supposed to fix this. This is just the way I am."

Are you as confused as I am? What the hell is he talking about? What does he mean he doesn't understand what to do? You just told him what you needed. What does he mean he doesn't understand how to fix this? It's simple. He can pick up the dang phone and call you. That's it. It doesn't get any easier than that.

Listen to me. When you're flat out explaining to him what you're looking for and he responds to you in a way that says he wasn't listening or doesn't care, that means he's not serious about you or he's not ready for the relationship. Either way, you don't need to stick around waiting for him to come around. It's a waste of your time. Plain and simple.

As I've stressed in previous chapters already, always make sure you communicate the issue to him before taking any action. You always want to make sure you address whatever is bothering you in a calm and loving manner. I will never encourage you to lash out at him or come off as attacking when addressing your issues. Even if you think he's a liar. Going into the conversation, if you think he's a liar, then that means the issue is bigger than what you're addressing in that moment. There's a larger problem present, a lack of trust.

Let's leave that alone for the moment. Again, always strive to communicate with him in a calm and loving manner when you express your concerns and needs. As I've said before, how he handles that will tell you everything you need to know. If he's not willing to embrace how you feel and do something about it, if he's not open to correcting his behavior and what's in his control, there's a problem.

If you're thinking to yourself, "Well, maybe I should just keep loving him and pouring into him and doing for him, it will help him come around. Eventually, he'll show me the love I need in return."

Wrong. Listen, your loving him is not going to be enough. Here's why: "You'll never be good enough for the wrong person." If you're dealing with the wrong man, then loving him is not the cure. Take a moment and consider this, ask yourself, "Do we even have a deep and genuine connection?"

If you follow my **Stephan Speaks** podcast or me on social media, you know I'm big on genuine connection being a necessary part of a successful relationship. If you don't have that, even if everything he says to you is true about his struggles and his issues, it won't matter. It won't matter because without a connection you guys aren't going to survive. The relationship isn't going to become what it needs to become.

Connection or not, the reality is that if he truly loves you the way he says he does, then trying and showing some progress should be easy for him regardless of his background or lack of experience. To be completely honest with you, it shouldn't be difficult for him. I'm not saying he's going to be perfect tomorrow. I'm not saying he's going to get everything right. What I'm saying is he should be showing a willingness to move in the right direction and put in the work. Again, he should be trying and showing progress toward correcting the issue so he's able to show you the love you need.

The only thing accepting his lack of effort, accepting his lack of action, and simply loving him will get you is hurt. He won't ever get to the point where he'll finally want to reciprocate your feelings and do for you because you've enabled his unloving behavior and you've given him permission to continue acting as he is used to acting with you. Again, this course of action is not going to work in your favor. Ever.

He'll have no reason to change. He'll have no reason to put in the hard work because even if it's a genuine issue that may include exploring some hurtful things from his past, that's difficult for most people to do. So, if he can avoid it, he's going to avoid it at all costs. Continuing to give him everything he wants and desires without him having to own up to or do anything on his part, is enabling him to keep taking advantage of the imbalance. The relationship will be lopsided, damaging, and draining for you.

You can support him and show him love as his friend. Friendship is the only acceptable dynamic left here. Even then I would still question, "Is he really the person you need to be supporting or not?" It goes back to whether there's a true connection there? Is he really being genuine about his position? Again, if he's genuine, he's going to show some effort. No effort means you should scratch the friendship. You don't even need to be his friend at that point. I was trying to give you an alternative route. Honestly, you don't even need to be his friend because you don't want to fall into any traps, he might be trying to set by keeping you around.

Be clear about what you're looking for. That is the only part you need to play. If you say to him, "I need you to hug me more." It doesn't take a rocket scientist to figure out how to hug you more. If you say to him, "I need you to be more considerate. I want you to think about me when you're out and about and check on me." Again, it doesn't take a rocket scientist to figure out how to do that. He can pick up the phone and call or text you. These are very clear and reasonable requests. The only reason a man won't embrace them and show a willingness to work on his issues is because he doesn't love you.

Ultimately, again, his words and actions must line up. When they don't, there's a problem. The problem needs to be explored and addressed. Once this happens, he needs to begin corrective action immediately. If there is no action taken, don't continue forward with him.

Too many times women are allowing situationships to drag on unnecessarily because they're not cutting things off when they need to be cut off. They're hoping for an improvement in behavior from someone who can't or is not willing to do better. The sooner you're able to recognize this and act, the happier you'll be.

One last point I want to make about him not showing his love but saying he loves you. Even though I explained at length how a man could have issues, the reality could also be that he has none. The above example doesn't apply to every man. There are men out here who have no problem saying whatever you want to hear. In most of these situations that's really what's going on. He's telling you what you want to hear. I hate to say it, but a smart man knows that the right words can make a woman weak for him. The right words can make her become putty in his hands. A lot of men know that if they just tell a woman they love her, they'll get a lot further with her that way.

Is it right? No. Is it beneficial to the man? Yes.

Arguably many men have grasped this concept and don't have a problem telling you what you want to hear. However, that's all it is. Empty words. Again, if his actions don't line up with his words, a lie is being told somewhere. Words and actions must line up with one another. Just like in the chapter where he says, "He doesn't want a girlfriend, but acts like your boyfriend." This is a similar situation. Except this time, he's telling you the right thing but doing the opposite, which cancels out his words.

Make sure his actions align with his words. You can't just rely solely on one or the other to evaluate how serious a man is about you. I would say there should be a higher priority put on his actions over his words. However, you really need both and they both need to compliment the other vs. canceling each other out. His actions must back up his words.

Too many people are experiencing a lot of damage and fatigue from dating and relationships simply because they've been in too many unhealthy, pointless, even toxic situations. Save yourself from going through these negative cycles. Abort the pointless missions sooner. Don't drag it out. Don't hold on because you're scared to be alone. Once you quickly recognize, "This isn't for me, this isn't going to work," don't talk yourself back into it. Get out of there with the quickness.

Now that you know what constitutes some of the nonsense, recognize it, address it, and if it's not corrected, move on. If we're all honest, we're all recovering from something.

You deserve both his spoken and expressed love through his actions in a way that lines up with your needs. No excuses.

He,
"Won't Let You Go, but That Doesn't Mean He Loves You"

*H*ave you ever met a man who seems to have it all together, but once you're in a relationship with him, you realize he doesn't know how to treat you? In addition to not knowing how to treat you, he refuses to let you move on even though it's clear to the both of you that the relationship isn't working?

Meet Kate. Kate found herself in this exact situation once she began dating Justin. During the dating phase, everything went as expected. Things were looking great and Kate felt like Justin was the total package. He courted her properly and a relationship developed. She was enjoying the attention and affection that he was giving her consistently. She secretly began letting her thoughts wonder into the possibility that Justin could be the real deal.

Fast forward six months. Kate and Justin's relationship began turning down a very, dark, bumpy road. Justin began disrespecting her. They argued a lot and things just took a turn for the worst.

Between you and me, there were red flags to begin with, but it wasn't enough to cause Kate to think that things would begin to blow up in her face, so suddenly, only after six months. However, she found herself trying to look over too many incidents. Justin had a temper. He also had a habit of taking out his work and life frustrations on her, the more comfortable he got within the relationship. The incidents began to pile up, one on top of the other. She lost count. The constant arguing, the constant going back and forth, his being disrespectful was weighing Kate down. Their relationship had hit a major snag and it was getting out of hand.

After putting up with the downturn of their relationship for another two months, Kate finally decided, "You know what, I can't do this anymore. Clearly, he must not love me because he doesn't respect me. He doesn't do what I need him to do. I'm going to end the relationship."

She decides to tell Justin it's over. He responded to her ending it, by lashing out at her. He showed no remorse or desire to reconcile and try to keep the relationship intact. Realizing she couldn't win the final argument and didn't care, she removed herself from the situation and was looking forward to being newly single.

A few days go by, Justin sends her a text. A few days after that he calls her and continues to call until she picks up. He wants another chance. The begging and pleading began. He was relentless with it. He says things are going to be different. Things are going to get better. He promises her he is going to do right this time.

Kate takes him back.

They try again. A month goes by. No incidents. However, by month two, he starts up again with wanting to argue all the time and starts back up with the disrespectful behavior. It constantly ended up being an issue of some kind with him that he felt he could take out on her.

They break up again.

This time though, during an argument, he ends up breaking up with her. Kate didn't expect it. She didn't like it. She was hurt. Let's face it, no one likes getting dumped. She just figured, she wouldn't sweat it. She was done with him this time for good and now he confirmed it by breaking up with her. Cool.

A week later, he's at it again. Begging and pleading for her to take him back.

This pretty much remains the cycle. They're together. They get into too many arguments. She leaves. He leaves. He comes back. Justin always came back no matter who broke it off.

In one of our coaching sessions, I remember Kate telling me, she wasn't sure anymore how to get off the emotional rollercoaster that was their relationship. She wasn't sure if she needed to let go once and for all or if the fact that he kept coming back, the fact that he was trying so hard despite all the mess-ups, was proof that he really loved her. She wasn't sure if he just didn't know how to handle the relationship and his emotions. This was the justification that other people were giving her and putting in her head for why she should consider staying in a relationship with Justin.

I shared with her the hard truth, "Just because he won't let you go, doesn't mean he loves you."

I've seen it repeatedly. Women will continue dealing with men who won't stop coming back, who won't leave them alone, even if these same men also don't treat them with the love and respect they deserve. They conclude that these types of men love them, but they don't. They equate the chasing with an overflow of love that doesn't exist.

If you've found yourself in this type of situation or close to it, I want to tell you the same thing I told Kate, "He doesn't love you. He's simply infatuated with you."

I can say that with the utmost certainty. Here's why:

It's easier to chase lust than it is to chase love. When a man is truly in love with a woman, he's not going to constantly behave in a toxic manner towards her. If there are instances where he messes up, he's not going to hesitate to figure out a way to correct his mistakes. However, he's also not going to let her go so easily with the "one minute we're together, the next minute we're not," game.

When you're in love with someone and they breakup with you or things blow up, if it gets to a point where you're being hurt repeatedly, you're not going to keep setting yourself up to be hurt repeatedly. Simply because it hurts too much. When you love a person, their mistakes, their wrongs, their disrespect, their negative words are going to cut you so much deeper than a person you're just lusting after.

In a lust-filled situation a person can and will keep taking a beating and come back to the person over and over again. I can honestly say, if this is his behavior, he doesn't really love you. Nope, it's infatuation. There is an unhealthy attachment there.

True love can't withstand this constant beating and punishment. It doesn't mean the person stops loving the other person. If you're truly in love with someone, you're going to love them, period, end of story. Even if you can't be with them, you will still love them. When you're still trying to be with them even though they keep pushing you away, doing you wrong, or acting out, that's not love.

Back to Justin. Again, when it's lust, it's easy to take the hit, get back up and return to the scene of the crime. Again, I'm speaking specifically of men here. When a man is pursuing a woman, if he just wants to have sex with her, he can take her rejection over and over unphased. I'm not saying every man, but there are plenty of men out there, who have no problem taking constant rejection. He'll keep coming back because he's obsessed with getting what he wants. His emotions aren't truly involved. He's not really in love here. He's not even really into you like that. It's become a game to him. You have become his conquest. He has no problem going full force and moving past any of your objections or obstacles.

Don't confuse that with love. Again, this man doesn't love you. Men who are truly in love with a woman, when they get pushed away, are much more easily discouraged and quicker to shut down. They're much more likely to give up. You're probably asking, "Why would he give up if he loves the woman?" Simple, because trying to hold on to her and the relationship will hurt a lot more than letting her go.

I'm not saying that every man in love immediately gives up. I'm not saying there has never been a man who hasn't constantly pursued a woman despite how much he was being hurt. Simply

because he was in love. What I'm saying is that
there's only so much a guy in love can take. Whereas
the man who isn't in love can take repeated
rejection and hurt with no problem.

Justin wasn't in love with Kate. He didn't have a
real connection with her either. It was evident by the
fact that he wasn't willing to do what was necessary
to change his behavior. If you want to argue and say
that he must've loved her because he kept coming
back, then why wouldn't he act right? Why
wouldn't he do right by her? Why wouldn't he learn
how to communicate properly? Why wouldn't he
figure out how to address his past issues? Why
wouldn't he confront his fear of commitment? Why
wouldn't he want to deal with whatever got in the
way of being the best man he could be for her and
making her happy?

Another reason why a man will keep coming back
is out of convenience. Kate, like so many other
women made it easy for Justin to come in and out
of the relationship, like a revolving door. When you
let him go, it's your job to not let him back in. It's
your job to keep shutting him down every time he
tries to get back in with you. It's your job to not

continuously give him the benefits of being with you, when technically he's not really with you because he's not fully committed to a relationship.

He knows if he calls you enough, texts you, pops up at your door, does the extra stuff, you'll eventually give in and that's all he's waiting for. He's just waiting for you to give in one more time. He's hoping to catch you in a vulnerable moment. He'll say what he knows you like to hear. He'll do whatever it takes to put a temporary smile on your face to manipulate you into taking him back. Even though he's still not going to do what he's supposed to do. He's hoping to wear you down into submission. It's convenient for him and less work than finding someone new to conquer.

When he gets you back, he doesn't even have to put in the full effort to stay around. His "good" behavior might last for a good month or two. Then it's going to be the same ole, same ole, becoming an on-going, never-ending cycle. It's going to be up to you to say, "No. Enough is enough." How you ask? Good question.

Let me give you some quick tips on closing the door completely.

Start by blocking his number. I know that sounds harsh, but it's necessary. Even though he's done you wrong repeatedly, you'll probably still have feelings for him. That's understandable. I'm not going to knock you for that, but if you know he's trying to call you, if you see his number, his name, it makes it harder for you to resist not picking up the phone. You don't want to weaken your stance in any way. You must take precautionary methods to help you stop the cycle.

Blocking his number is going to help you avoid talking to him and letting him back in. It's literally your first form of defense against his charm and manipulating actions. You can tell him right after you end it, "Hey, listen, you're going to be blocked so don't attempt to call or reach out to me again. The door is now shut for good." Then you keep it shut and don't open it back up. Blocking his number is a must.

Next, don't entertain conversation under any circumstances. Let's say he just pops up on you at your job, don't get into a dialogue with him. He isn't saying anything new. He isn't telling you what you haven't already heard before. It's the same script.

The same lines repeatedly. You've already heard his sob story, so why even engage? Why go back and forth? Why argue?

One of the biggest mistakes you can make is getting into an argument and going back and forth with someone you've already ended it with. You feel the need to defend yourself. Before you know it, the back and forth with him psychologically reels you back into the situation. He's getting you emotionally invested with him again. It's a mind game. So, stop it before it even starts.

Now, if by some chance, a miracle happens and he has a come to Jesus moment, then it might be worth hearing him out. Maybe suddenly he figures out, he's been a jerk and wants to correct it. If this is the case, I'm not completely against you're hearing him out. However, you'll be able to see it right away. You'll be able to sense the difference in him. When a man has truly changed, when he's truly grown, his energy is different. The way he presents himself is going to have changed. I think as a woman; your intuition will be able to sense it.

However, let's be real, in majority of situations that's not what happens. Nothing will have changed.

It's unlikely that he's going to get it together. Not impossible, just not likely.

The last thing you need to do to shut the door for good is remove any influences of him in your life. What I mean by that is, if you all are friends on social media, unfriend him and block him so he can't cyber stalk you. After you unfriend and block him, don't go lurking on his pages either. Avoid looking at his social media. You don't want to have anything that's going to trigger an emotional response from you and cause you to want to fall back into the situationship and negative cycle.

Be mindful of your triggers with him and guard yourself from them. The fact is, he won't let you go, but you need to stop letting him stay. He has no reason to let you go. The reality is, you provide some form of benefit to him and he wants to keep it. Whether it's a place to stay, money, stability, food, sex, whatever the case may be. He isn't going to be willing to give you what you need and you're not demanding it because you allow him to do nothing and still benefit.

It's like if a job is willing to pay you $400 just for showing up to work. Why would you let that go? You have every reason to try your best to get that job back every time you mess up. You're not going to say, "Well, since I don't know how to do the job, let me just give it a rest, and let it go." Nope, if you think you can find a way back in and still get that $400 check just for showing up to work, you're going to try your hardest to get back in. This is his mentality. If he can keep getting back in with minimal effort and once, he's there, reap all the benefits of what you provide, then why the hell not? The only person not benefitting in this situation is you.

You might be thinking, "Isn't it better to have someone than no one at all? I don't like being alone and all these other guys are worthless." Wrong. I need you to remove the false perceptions and fears you're holding on to. They're paralyzing you and causing you to stay in a perpetually toxic situation.

Your fears and false perceptions are screwing with your ability to see clearly. This man is not for you. Things are not going to get better if there are no real consequences. Your breaking up with him for a few weeks, a month, those aren't real consequences. Deep down he still knows he can come back. He knows he has you in his back pocket so-to-speak. Bottom line. He's going to use that to his advantage repeatedly.

Instead of spending any more time and energy on him, start focusing on you.

Focus on working on improving yourself and doing the things that bring you joy and happiness, not drama and pain. This man is dead weight in your life, and he's going to drown or suffocate you if you let him. He's stopping you from living your best life, being happy, and reaching your full potential. He's not supposed to be there in the first place. However, it's up to you to remove him and to let go. Once you do, keep that door closed.

Again, just because he won't let you go, doesn't mean he loves you. I know it's tough to accept. I know it's quite possible you've made a significant time investment with this man. It's never easy to let something go and walk away when you have put time, energy, and true feelings into it. However, it needs to happen.

Walking away from him is what's best. Walk away and don't look back. You have a lot to look forward to. The truth is, you hold all the power in the situation. Once you understand that, you'll be able to walk in that power. You'll be able to find peace with the situation sooner. You'll be able to start moving in the direction you need to and the possibility of meeting someone who is right for you increases.

It's up to you. You have the strength to do it. Look within you and make it happen. Stay strong. Stay focused. Take your power back. Move forward in confidence. Remember, you're in control here.

He Says, "He's Separated and Getting a Divorce"

*M*eet Andrea.

"I need your help. I'm facing a very difficult situation. I'm not sure what to do."

"Okay. Well, tell me what's going on?" I replied.

"Well, I've been dating this guy for two years. I really love him. I think he loves me too. I really want to be able to move forward with him."

"Well, what's the problem? What's holding you guys back?" I asked.

"Well, technically he's still married."

"He's still technically married?" I replied, trying to control the worry in my voice.

"Yeah. Well, you know, they're separated, and they're supposed to get a divorce, but it hasn't happened yet."

"Okay. Tell me a little bit more about the situation."

Before I share more of Andrea's story, I want to pause here to answer your doubt on the time frame. You might be thinking to yourself, "Two years? Why in the world would she stick around waiting for a man that's still married. Listen, this is real life and this type of situation is more common than you might think. Time flies. Before you know it, two or three years have gone by and you're still in the waiting position.

Back to Andrea. She goes on to explain how they met. They had been hanging out consistently even though he's always a little restricted on time and when he can see her due to his being busy with his kids for the weekends, etc. I continued to listen to her story through to the end.

"So, what should I do? How should I handle this situation? How should I proceed?" she asked.

"Well, Andrea," I started off by making the obvious very clear. "If he's separated, then he's still married."

Please understand something here, if you desire to be married one day, then you always need to respect other people's marriages. You can't afford to go around trying to play the "technical" game with other people's relationships because you're caught up in what you want at that moment.

I get it. Divorce can be tricky. It can take a long time. It can be dragged out for a number of reasons on either side. In some situations, the couple are genuinely separated and genuinely have no plans on getting back together. However, I'll repeat myself here. "If he's separated, he's still married." This is dangerous ground to be walking on.

Let's just say, for example, the guy is telling the truth about being genuinely separated but the divorce is complicated. There could be a lot of financial aspects that cause problems for him and he's trying to work everything out so that he doesn't come out of it with the short end of the stick. Again, it happens. He could be genuinely telling the truth in this case.

However, if he still has what he's looking for on the side with you, then he has no reason to pick up the pace and get the deal done quicker. People will let divorces drag on as long as you allow them to. If they're getting their needs met, why rush? Why put himself through the extra turmoil, the trouble, the hassle? He can just let things drag on. He can do his thing on the side with you and not have any urgency in the situation.

I've known people who've ended up being separated for years, several years before ever getting a divorce finalized. You never know how long a divorce is going to drag out. Again, it's very dangerous to entertain a "technically still married" man.

Now, you might be reading this and thinking, "Well, I would never mess with a married man, separated or not. I would never bother with this kind of a situation." You're preaching to the choir. I hear you. Good for you if you wouldn't entertain it. However, before you feel like you can skip this chapter because you don't think it would be beneficial to you. I know plenty of women who have found themselves in this very situation who also thought they would never be in it.

I'm not questioning your position here. However, you never know what you may find yourself in. You just never know. Sometimes a woman doesn't go into it knowingly, willingly wanting to date a married or currently separated man. The woman might have been led to believe he was available and not in a relationship at all. What happens? The woman gets close, feelings get involved, and she becomes emotionally attached to him before finding out the true story.

This is a non-judgement zone. I want you to be prepared no matter what.

When this type of situation occurs and the woman finds out after she's fallen for the guy, that he's still technically married, it can be a struggle to walk away from it. This can happen to anyone, even someone with the best intentions of not getting caught up in this type of scenario. I want you to be mindful of looking for the red flags if you ever do find yourself in this situation.

One of the main reasons why this is such a dangerous situation for you to be in is because things can change for the worse at any moment, without warning. When I say, "change for the worse," I'm talking about you being left out in the cold, feelings and all, if the separation turns out to become a reconciliation.

I've seen plenty of situations where married couples were separated, on the verge of divorce, and at the last second, right before they signed the papers, something happens and the next thing you know, they want to work it out. Now, you may be saying, "Oh, absolutely not. It couldn't just happen out of nowhere. They must've been talking about it or they were never really separated."

No. There are situations where people are genuinely separated and in the process of divorcing and then something happens that turns the whole situation around. It could be guilt because of the kids. It could be because they find out the financial ramifications are too difficult to deal with. It could be a rekindling of the flame. It could be anything. Yes, it happens.

If you're the other woman, you don't know what's going to happen from one moment to the next. You're also not as in the loop as you may think or hope to be because he isn't going to give you every detail of the process of his divorce. Even if he was willing to tell you everything, sometimes the unexpected can still happen at the drop of a dime.

Entertaining a married man who is separated and currently waiting for that divorce to be finalized, means you're playing with fire. Like majority of women who've been in this situation before you, you'll end up getting burned.

If he's serious about getting his divorce, then he needs to get his divorce. Now, I don't want you to think I'm promoting divorce. I don't want you to think I encourage divorce. Not at all. However, if a couple is already at that stage and it's going to happen, let it happen first before you start entertaining him. Let him do what he needs to do. Let him close out that chapter in his life before he tries to begin a new one with you.

I've seen situations where there was a genuine connection between the separated man and the new woman because let's be honest here, everyone doesn't marry the right person the first time around. Some people will marry a person they have no connection with at all and then wonder why the marriage didn't work out. It's very possible that as the other woman you could have real feelings for him. The connection between the two of you could be electric and it could honestly turn into something amazing one day.

However, it's not the time to pursue it. You should not entertain feelings for him because he's still married. I'm not even going to say technically because there is no technical.

Separated still means married.

Until he's divorced, until those papers are signed, done, stamped by the judge or whatever happens at the courthouse when you get a divorce, this man is still married. Ignoring it doesn't change the facts.

Andrea ignored the facts and found herself caught between a rock and a hard place. In her situation, he wasn't lying. He was separated and the divorce did finally happen. However, after almost three years of Andrea waiting, once he was divorced, he realized he wasn't ready to get right back into another serious relationship. Andrea ended up walking away feeling like it was a huge waste of her time. Not to mention hurt because while she was waiting, she invested all her feelings and energy into him. She just knew it was going to work out once he divorced. In the end, it didn't.

Now that we've explored the scenario where the man in the situation was being genuine and honest.

Let's explore the possibility that the man in this situation could also be lying.

Again, every guy who is separated is not lying about everything. However, I must be real here. Being the third party and the one in the dark often, is too risky of a situation to put yourself in. You are at the mercy of the situation and you are left in this grey area not knowing what's really coming.

Let me give you another example. Meet Tonya, also a well-intentioned other woman. Tonya was dating a married man who was separated and who claimed he was getting a divorce. To my knowledge the guy was dating a couple women while still married. However, Tonya thought she was number one on the totem pole and that everything would go her way. She even went as far as to allow herself to get pregnant by this man. I'm using the word 'allow' intentionally here because she knew exactly what she was doing. It was her plan all along and she thought she'd won the lottery because she was going to have this guy's baby. Somehow, she figured her pregnancy solidified her spot. She thought that once he left his wife, he would be with her and her alone to raise their child together.

Well, guess what? He never divorced his wife. He never had any intentions of truly being with Tonya exclusively, even after she got pregnant by him. I don't know if when it all came out, the wife stuck around. I'm not sure. I do know that he didn't leave her willingly, if it did get to that. I'm willing to bet they probably didn't get a divorce because if he was doing all that messing around on the side, she was probably already accepting a lot of his indiscretion even before Tonya's situation occurred. Women are smart. Women have an idea when things are going down and when they aren't right.

I shared that story to simply say you can't bank on the guy leaving his wife either way. Getting involved with a married man, separated or not, will lead to broken promises and wasted time. He can say, "I'm going to do this," and "I'm going to do that. The divorce is going to happen, just wait a few more months." However, it's likely he'll keep extending the few months. In the meantime, he's still married, and you'll continue to be his side chick, mistress, girlfriend, whatever. You'll continue to give him the benefits of you, your love, your time, and everything that you have. You'll continue to pour into the relationship as if it was under normal circumstances.

However, it's not a normal situation. Acting like it is will lead you to shooting yourself in the foot. If he's that serious about you, if he's that serious about getting his divorce, then you don't need to keep giving and waiting. Broken promises and wasted time are a very damaging situation for you to be in. You don't need to give so much to him, thinking he's eventually going to leave his wife, and then it never happens.

I want you to ask yourself something. If you are in this situation, Why? Why are you holding on?

Ask yourself that question because I need to bring the accountability factor in here. Sure, he has a responsibility here but so do you. Too many times people like to point the finger at the man and the female party in this situation likes to play the victim. However, neither approach is healthy. I believe in both parties accepting responsibility for their part.

Saying that to say that I've seen a lot of women be willing to entertain a married man not because its true love involved, not because he's truly the best man for them, but simply because it's a dynamic that allows them to have companionship without needing to be vulnerable. Since he's still married, the marriage serves as a kind of buffer.

Buffers are a way to not allow yourself to fully dive into the emotional aspect of a relationship while still being able to enjoy relationship benefits like: companionship, intimacy, having someone to spend time with, etc. Now, this point only applies to women who knew what they were getting themselves into from the very beginning. It's one thing if you didn't know. But when you know, you've got to ask yourself, "Why am I entertaining this?"

Be honest with yourself.

Even if the situationship starts off casual and you're not emotionally invested, you can still find yourself caught up in the end. You can still find yourself becoming emotionally attached to a certain degree and struggling to walk away after things take a turn toward reconciliation. Again, not because he's the best man for you, but because this was a comforting situation. It created a type of comfort zone for you. It was easy for you to hold on to because you didn't have to put yourself completely out there.

Bottom line, he's still married, which means he's not available. You have no idea if he's really going to get a divorce and you don't need to hang around waiting to see either. Whether real feelings are involved or not, respect his marriage.

As I said at the beginning of the chapter, if you want a great relationship, if you aspire to marriage one day in your own life, then respect other people's marriages. Let me also add, don't be so quick to believe everything he says about his wife.

Again, I'm not here to man bash. I'm not saying every man on the brink of a divorce is feeding people lies and not being genuine about the facts of his marriage. Some men have been legitimately tortured in their marriages. Some men have been married to women who treated them horribly. I don't deny that in any way.

However, I've also seen tons of situations where a guy will feed the new woman all kinds of false information to gain sympathy and to paint his partner as the wicked witch, when that isn't exactly how it went down. You, as the other woman in that situation, start to believe the hype and you start to develop a hatred or anger or saltiness towards the wife.

Bottom line. She didn't do anything to you. She doesn't owe you anything either because she's the wife.

Respect her position.

Whether she's the right wife or the wrong wife, she's still the current wife. You must ask yourself, "How would I want to be treated if I were in the same situation?" If nothing else, you would want to be respected in this situation. Period. Show respect for her because honestly you don't know her and it's not your place to judge her.

If you have friends or family entertaining situations like this, let them know what's up. Let them know the truth about the different risks their facing by staying in this type of situation.

Again, not in a judgmental way because that's not the point here. Sure, people are going to do what they want to do, but the more we speak out about these types of situations not being acceptable, the more dialogue we have around this topic, the more we discourage it. We need to not act like it's all good when people are engaging in relationships with individuals who are still married. The more we talk about it and put the facts out here, the more it'll become taboo. The less acceptable it will be.

Women need to be reminded of their worth and supported emotionally. Not judged.

You're worth more than accepting an indefinite position as a side chick. You're better than that.

Again, if he's separated and says he's getting a divorce, he's still married. Leave him alone.

He Says,
"God Told Him You're His Wife"

*M*eet Nancy. Nancy met Mark at a church function. He was a good-looking guy, tall, nice build, great smile. Mark caught Nancy's eye and stood out to her. He initiated a conversation. They hit it off and decided to exchange numbers. They continued to get to know each other, regularly talking for extended periods on the phone. Things seemed to be going well and they had a good vibe.

Despite the good vibes, there were some things that Nancy noticed about Mark that might become an issue, but she figured maybe she was being too picky. Overall, she really liked him. He seemed like a great guy. She didn't want to harp on the little things. She decided to look past them and not let them bother her and to keep moving forward with Mark.

A month passed by. On their weekly date night that they'd begun having since meeting, Mark says to Nancy,

"I prayed about you and us. God told me that you're my wife."

Mark's sudden confession made Nancy very happy and excited to hear.

Nancy was 37, and prior to meeting Mark, was reaching a point where she was starting to lose hope in relationships. She started wondering if she would really find the man God has for her, get married, and finally be free from the woes of single life. She felt like her time was running out, so to speak.

"Oh my gosh. Finally! Here it is. Here's my chance to reach the level I've always desired from a relationship. Marriage! To have somebody and to move forward. Mark's a man of God, he's a believer. We met at a church function. He's prayed about us and God told him, I'm his wife. This is awesome."

Of course, Nancy didn't say any of this out loud to Mark, but she was ecstatic. They continued to move forward, and a serious relationship developed. Once they transitioned into something a little more serious, they spent more time together. The month after Mark's confession things remained consistent within their progressing relationship. They hadn't really talked anymore about God's revelation or what it meant, and they weren't discussing wedding plans either.

At the beginning of month two of their committed relationship, four months after meeting, things started to go downhill. Nancy started to see a different side of Mark. She started noticing very controlling behavior. Mark suddenly wanted to regulate what she wore, where she went, and who she talked to. She also began experiencing a more verbally aggressive side of Mark. He started talking down to her and being disrespectful in the way he spoke to her.

Mind you, Mark also quoted Bible scriptures, went to church with her, and played it off like nothing was going on. On the surface it appeared that he was a man of God, but his behavior behind closed doors was the complete opposite.

Believe it or not, Nancy still convinced herself and believed the relationship could work. After all, Mark did tell her that God told him she was his wife. She figured that maybe in time things would work out. She remained in the relationship.

Be careful about listening to a man who tells you God told him you are his wife because, simply put, he could be the devil in disguise.

Listen, just because a guy goes to church, quotes scripture, yells, "Praise God. Hallelujah. Amen," doesn't mean he is of God. It doesn't mean he's truly walking with God and has a genuine relationship with Him. Unfortunately, there are men out here who are using God and spirituality as game to get women. They're using a pro-God mask to disguise their evil intentions or their despicably toxic ways because they know it wins the trust of women.

Listen, that isn't to say every man who has ever said that God led him to you or that he prayed about you is lying. However, you need to be a bit wary of a guy that says this to you. Don't be so quick to jump on the bandwagon because he's saying all the right things from a spiritual perspective.

As I've already mentioned countless times throughout this book, it's not just about his words, his actions must line up as well. If you want to take a spiritual or biblical approach to things, the Bible says, *"Yes, just as you can identify a tree by its fruit, so you can identify people by their actions."* Matthew 7:20

It goes back to you trusting your intuition. Listening to your spirit will help you be more discerning when it comes to people and help you learn how to pick up on things that may put you in harm's way.

Understand that there are a lot of manipulative people living in this world and the God route is a great way to manipulate women. If a man claims to have a strong spiritual relationship with God, you need to pay attention to what he does outside of church, church functions, and church people. How does he treat you around others compared to when other people aren't around? Is his behavior consistent? How does he treat other people? How does he talk to people? Is he a loving, generous person? Is he patient?

These are the signs that will show you if he is truly a man of God or not. There are plenty of people in the church, men and women, who claim to be Godly, saying all the right things, but who are secretly wicked, judgmental, nasty and negative. I'm not saying this in a judgmental way either. I say it as an observation and what I have witnessed for myself from a place of humility and clothed in God's grace. Knowing that, allows me to understand and accept the imperfection in others.

High and mighty church folk are often among the extremely flawed human beings of the world because they don't understand the error of their ways in looking down their noses at others. They don't understand how toxic their behavior is because some of them grew up in this type of dysfunction. If they grew up in "church environments" that involved people praising and singing in the building, then going outside of church and acting less-than-holy in their everyday lives, like God isn't all-knowing, then they might not realize how they really are.

Let's consider for a second that this guy is telling the truth. Maybe he has prayed. Maybe you're dealing with a man who has a great relationship with God, who has prayed about you, and genuinely has heard or at the very least genuinely believes God has told him you're his wife.

Again, if someone truly has a relationship with God, it should reflect in the way they're walking in life. It doesn't mean they're going to be perfect. If you've read my book, *The Man God Has for You*, I stress the fact that a man can be a man of God, really love God, but it doesn't mean he's going to be a perfect guy. It doesn't mean he won't do anything wrong. It doesn't mean he won't have his down moments.

There's a difference between someone who is consistently good and has his slip-ups vs. the person who is consistently bad and then sprinkles in a few good moments. Sprinkling a few moments of good doesn't make him a man you should trust, listen to, or be in a relationship with. A man who is consistently good and makes honest mistakes or has honest struggles, that's totally different.

He could have heard from God and talks to God. I do believe that we can talk to God and get answers when we pray. There are people who are in tune spiritually and in close relationship with God that seek God in their lives for guidance. It's not far-fetched at all. I know a ton of true stories of men who have met a woman of genuine interest, prayed about her, and God said it was their wife, and they ended up marrying the woman.

When a man says that God told him that you're his wife, ask yourself, "Do we even have real a connection?"

Are you even feeling him in that way at all? Because if you don't feel the same way and aren't on that level with him, then what he says makes no difference. Even if you want to argue, maybe you're just not seeing it yet. Okay, fine, maybe you need more time. I would then say, don't proceed with any talk about getting serious or getting married until that time comes.

Don't sit there and take his word for it just because he seems like he would be honest, like he wouldn't lie, or because you're in a hurry to have a relationship and get married. Don't take his word for it because you want so badly to believe he's telling you the truth. You can't afford to get caught up in that. Understand that everything must line up to back up that word.

If you are indeed his wife, as he says God told him, then a genuine connection should exist. There should be a mutual attraction present. There should be real feelings on your end that indicate to you, okay, this could be real. In addition to all that, you also need to go one step deeper. You also need to have your own connection with God and get confirmation on his claim.

Let me tell you something. It doesn't matter if it's a man telling you, you're his wife, a pastor prophesying over you, or church members giving you a good word based on what they feel is good, loving advice. These people aren't God. You still must have your own relationship where you go to God directly and verify what's being told to you.

Go to God yourself in prayer and ask for verification, "Hey God. Is such-n-such supposed to be my husband? God is our connection real? Is this the relationship you want me to embrace? Is this who you want me to be with?" Then you need to wait and listen for God to give you the green light. If not, it doesn't make sense moving forward with him.

Now, you might be thinking, "Well, I don't know if I can hear God," or "I don't ever hear God speaking to me," or "When I do pray about these things, I don't get a clear answer."

As far as listening to and hearing from God goes, I will give you one tip. When you ask God a question in prayer, ask with the expectation to receive the answer right there. What I mean by this is that a lot of times when we pray, we either pray to just make a request, we pray to vent, or we pray to thank God for something. Don't get me wrong, all those things are cool, but a lot of times we don't pray and ask a specific question to receive a specific answer. On top of that, when we do ask a question, we ask it in a very passive way.

Like, "God, show me the answer to this." Basically, God hit me over the head randomly and give me a sign or something that tells me what to do."

The problem with this approach is, once you leave that prayer, you switch to being on high alert looking for any sign that might tell you something and leaving it up to you to interpret that sign. Essentially, now you're left guessing. "Did this mean that?" "Did that mean this?"

Overanalyzing everything will drive you crazy. Not only will you drive yourself crazy, you still don't really know if anything that you're paying attention to is really the sign. You still don't really know what

God is telling you about the man or the relationship. As a result, you're ultimately going to come to your own conclusion or make your own assumptions to get your answer. That's not the most effective or right way to go about it in my opinion.

When you pray and you ask God a question, you must ask with the expectation that you're going to hear God answer you right then, right there in your spirit. The Bible says, "*Ask and you shall receive.*" Matthew 7:8, NLT

Make your request. Sit still. Listen intently for God's answer. It really boils down to learning how to tap into your intuition. I do believe that people's intuition is their spirit speaking to them. When you pray, you are essentially going into a quiet room with your spirit and getting in direct communication with it. Tapping into your intuition, your inner voice will tell you what you need to do.

You've got to clear your mind to hear it though. You've got to surrender yourself to whatever the answer is because if you go in trying to hear a specific answer, you're going to block your ability to get the correct answer. You'll make it very hard for yourself. Instead, really open yourself up, surrender your will, and listen.

Trust me. This is going to help you. This is going to help you immensely because again, I've seen many women go down this path of listening to what some man told them. Claiming that God said this, that, and the other. When they do this, they're ultimately headed for disaster. You need to have your own relationship with God. You must be able to go to God yourself and ask Him to verify what someone else has told you.

The bottom line, there are going to be some genuine guys and there are going to be some manipulative ones. I want to share a quote someone once said to me because it rings true here. "When God brings you the original, the devil will always bring you an imposter." Meaning, when that right guy comes into your life, a lot of times, some other guy is going to come around and that other guy is there to distract you. That other guy is meant to completely take you off your path and it's going to be hard to figure out who is who because they look very similar.

It's not clear who comes first. Sometimes the imposter comes right before the original. Sometimes the original comes, and the imposter follows shortly after. I've seen it time and time again. When the imposter comes, he talks some good game. He does the things that make you think he's the most logical choice.

Again, that's why you need to learn to talk to God and tap into your spiritual intuition because, in that moment, you're going to be confused and conflicted. You're going to, for different reasons, be fearful, emotionally confused, and torn. You will possibly be drawn to the wrong guy. The imposter will try to get the best of you because it'll make more sense on the surface for him to be the one and it's easier to just go with that. However, that's the wrong choice. You need to learn how to tap into the truth within, by having your own spiritual relationship and talking to God for yourself.

Practice trusting your intuition and inner guidance, which is always going to guide you into the best outcomes for you. Also pray for a heightened spirit of discernment, this will set you up for the best results, not just in relationships, but overall throughout every area of your life.

Three Reasons Why
He Lies

———◦◉◦———

A question I get from women all the time, and one of the main reasons I wrote a book like this in the first place is, "Why do men lie? Why do they have to lie so much? As if honesty just doesn't exist in their DNA. Do they not have any concept or grasp of what being truthful and transparent is all about?" Well, technically that's more than one question, but the basis of them all deals around the chronic lies some men tell.

Lies create a lot of confusion, damage, and unhealthy attachments to be quite honest with you. I really felt women needed an understanding as to the reasoning behind the lies that some men tell. There's really a very simple truth to this. Before I get to that simple truth, I want to fully explain the reasoning behind all the lies. There are really three main reasons why a man will blatantly lie to you.

First, he can't get what he wants by telling you the truth. Let me give you an example. You might hear some women say, "If a man would just admit all he wants is sex, then maybe he'll get it." What they're saying is if he's honest, he might get rewarded for his honesty and get what he wants. They're saying that basically the nonsense can be avoided altogether if he's upfront from the beginning about what he really wants.

Let me start by saying that it sounds good in theory. I'm not going to say that this isn't the case for some women. In some situations, a man could just be completely honest saying he just wants sex and he'll get it. It can happen.

However, most men have already concluded—the real conclusion, might I add—that more times than not being straightforward and honest about what he wants is not going to get you to have sex with him. Plain and simple. If men thought they could get what they wanted by simply telling you what they wanted, then they would do it without a doubt. It would be easier and less complicated for everyone involved.

Let me be clear. I'm in no way validating the lies some men tell. I'm also not trying to make excuses for their lies. What I'm trying to do is make it plain and explain to you the reasoning behind the lies in case you've ever found yourself confused or frustrated by a lie a man has told you. I feel it's important for you to have full clarity on what contributes to this type of behavior.

Again, some men lie because they don't think they can get what they want by telling you the truth. These men are going to do what they feel they must do to achieve their desired outcome. Whether the outcome they want is sex. Whether it's getting money out of you, free meals, free housing, you name it. At the end of the day it boils down to human nature. When I say human nature, I mean that men and women, people of all types lie because they want a desired outcome and they fear they can't achieve that outcome with the truth.

Be honest with yourself. Haven't you taken this same approach at one time or another? Again, I'm not condoning the behavior or saying it's acceptable, but once you understand the why behind it, then hopefully you won't be weighed down by the stress of all the lies. Too many times you're sitting there wondering, analyzing, overthinking about why he lied, and it simply boils down to the fact that he couldn't get what he wanted by telling you the truth. It's simple. Stop overthinking it.

Another reason for a man to lie is if he thinks you can't handle the truth. I understand it's unfair for a man to jump to that conclusion. At the very least he should give you the opportunity to decide for yourself and determine what you want to do with the truth. However, as much as I encourage people to be honest and transparent, I've talked to a lot of different men and one of the biggest complaints they have is that their woman can't handle the truth.

Let's use how you look to him as an example. You're in a relationship. You all are getting ready for an event and you ask him, how something looks on you, if it looks good, or if what you have on is unflattering?

He may genuinely feel like what you chose to wear is unflattering and does not like it. If he thought he could be honest and say how he really felt without it turning into an issue, he would gladly tell you the truth. However, he's probably already experienced the effects of his truth not aligning with what you want to hear, or he's learned from other men, that lying to you about those types of questions is better for him and the relationship. It could also be because he doesn't want to hurt your feelings. He will lie instead of hurting your feelings and having you be mad at him for being honest. Men really do fear the repercussions of their honesty.

This reasoning can be applied to so many different situations. Some men are willing and ready to be honest with you, but they're paralyzed by the fear of how you're going to respond to that honesty. It's important for you to realize this. If you want to get more truth out of a man, you need to be smart about how you react in the moment. Your reaction will determine his course of action in the future. When he sees and understands you can handle honesty, he'll be honest. If you don't jump down his throat because his honest opinion to your question was something that you didn't like, if you handle it correctly, he'll trust you with his honesty.

If you don't lash out or let your emotions get the best of you in the moment, his willingness to be honest with you will increase exponentially.

Now, yes, he should be willing to be honest on his own no matter what but put yourself in his shoes for a second. It's probably happened to you. Maybe with your mother, siblings, friends, or in a previous relationship, there've been moments where you were asked for your honesty, you gave it, and you got penalized for being honest. Either you were attacked, the person caught an attitude, or there was another result, it was all because you were being honest and truthful in answering their question.

How did that cause you to view telling them the truth in the future? It probably made you not want to be as honest anymore with them because either you were fearful of their reaction or didn't want to deal with the backlash of it. You were probably more willing to lie or bend the truth or avoid the question altogether, instead of telling them the truth and bracing for the consequences. Some men are no different. If you don't learn how to handle these moments, you're increasing the chances of him answering your questions with lies vs. telling you the truth.

I feel I need to continue reminding you that this isn't to validate or condone the lies, I'm simply explaining what is going on behind them.

You want to show him, by your reaction, you're a woman who can and will be able to handle the truth when you ask for it. On the other hand, if you've shown that you know how to handle the truth and he still prefers to tell lies, it boils down to him being immature, insecure, and selfish. I don't say this to put the guy down or paint him out to be a monster. However, a lack of honesty is a sign of a lack of maturity, a lack of security, and an example of selfishness.

Again, if he's caught up in the moment of what he wants or what he wants to avoid or what he thinks is the preferred route to take, not considering the impact of the lie, it shows he's also not even considering you at all in this situation. It's not about protecting you, it's about protecting him and what's best for him at that moment and in the long run. Of course, when he lies, he's hoping he can get away with it. There's usually no full grasp on the impact the lie(s) will have when they finally come to the surface. Even though almost in every situation the lie eventually comes to the surface, mostly because men aren't the greatest liars. He'll still choose to lie vs. tell you the truth.

A lack of maturity, a lack of knowing how to effectively communicate, a lack of experience in healthy relationships—when I say healthy relationships, I mean his relationships in general—makes it likelier that a man will struggle in romantic relationships. If he doesn't have healthy relationships in his life, with friends, family, co-workers, etc., he's going to have a hard time in a romantic relationship because his feelings will be intensified, and he doesn't know how to properly handle them.

Understand that he's going to have a lot of growing pains, in terms of being able to really handle this current relationship in a mature fashion. I mentioned being immature as a reason why some men lie. I also need to mention insecurity as a reason for him lying. Sometimes men lie to hide their own flaws. The lies are meant to hide the things that we're afraid to expose about ourselves because we're worried about how we're going to be judged.

I say "how we" because I'm a man too, and it's not like I've never lied to a woman for the reason of wanting to cover up my own shortcomings. I'd be lying now, if I didn't include myself, period.

It's happened to the best of us for numerous reasons. Insecurity has a way of creeping up on people and when you truly like someone and vice versa, it can cause you both to hold back information. Let me give you an example.

I knew a guy who met a woman and instantly he was into everything about her. He really, really wanted to see where things could go and shortly after meeting her, he was already ready to take things to the next level. As I mentioned in an earlier chapter, it doesn't take the average man long to recognize the great potential in a woman as far as whether she could be his future wife? A lot of times women are conditioned to believe that it takes a man a long time to figure it out, it really doesn't.

Back to my example. He saw the potential in her instantly, but he had two children by two different women and because he really liked this woman, he was afraid to tell her this information upfront. He was genuinely afraid it would scare her off. He didn't want her to judge his situation without giving him a fair chance and allowing them to see if they had a mutual connection. So, he didn't tell her. He purposely kept that information out.

They continued getting to know each other and there was a mutual connection. She was also really into him. Everything was great. Thankfully, in this situation, he didn't let her find out about his children on her own. It's always worse when you find out about a lie yourself, instead of the other person fessing up. It doesn't make it better necessarily if someone tells you after feelings are involved, it's never the same as knowing in advance, but it's always worse when you find out on your own by accident.

In this situation, he ends up eventually coming clean on his own. Of course, she's hurt. Unfortunately, all it takes is one lie to ruin an otherwise perfectly good relationship. All it takes is one lie to plant a seed of doubt in your partner. In this case, it did hurt her, and it did have a negative impact on their relationship, but eventually they were able to move past it and work it out.

That story was an example to show you how a man will lie out of his own insecurity. His lie was out of the fear that she wouldn't accept him if he told her the full truth. It in no way justifies the situation. If he eventually comes clean then you then must choose whether to continue to roll with him, giving him the benefit of the doubt or not. At least he came clean. However, that's your choice. I just wanted to explain it because this is real life and it's reasoning behind why he sometimes lies or withholds information.

Again, one of the best things you can do if your desire is to eliminate or decrease the chances of lying occurring, is to show you are open-minded to things. An open mind doesn't mean you're going to agree with everything. It doesn't mean you're going to accept everything. It simply means you're going to be open to hearing him out and trying to see where he's coming from. You won't immediately jump down his throat or immediately jump to judge him. You'll keep your composure and communicate with love and patience. You'll show him that he can feel comfortable opening up to you and not have to worry about getting backlash from you, when he does share his truth with you. Even if it means eventually you decide not to move forward with him.

Creating a trusting, open, honest, environment within the dynamic of your interaction with a man will decrease the lies he tells. However, ultimately you don't have control over him. If he decides to not be truthful for any reason, that's on him. It'll be up to him to learn how to mature and grow up.

He must learn to get past his insecurities and be confident about who he is as a man and what he brings to the table. He needs to be willing to be unselfish and not be self-centered, only thinking about himself in the moment. Instead, he needs to be thinking about you and him and how his lie is going to impact the relationship going forward. He needs to man up.

In the end, you also need to make sure you're doing your part to create, encourage, and enhance an open and honest environment. Of course, that includes you being open and honest with him as well.

Ultimately people are going to lie if that's what they choose to do. I don't say people to let men off the hook. I say people to put things in perspective. In many of the situations that I've seen, many of the clients I've coached, women in general will often take the lie very, very personal, internalizing it.

"Why did he have to lie to me? Why can't he tell me the truth?"

His lie isn't an act against you. It's a part of human nature. It's a human flaw. It's a flaw that he has. It's not about you. It's about him being caught up in himself in the moment. Can we as individuals help create environments that are more honest? Absolutely. If you're going to demand honesty, then you must give honesty. If you want openness, you must be willing to be open. You can't be telling lies and then be mad at him for telling you lies as a result. Your actions set the stage for you to get back exactly what you're putting out.

As a woman, I truly believe you possess an intuition so strong that you can pick up on the smallest detail out of place in a man's story, behavior, etc. You can immediately tell when something is off. Men aren't the best liars. I honestly haven't ever felt like men ever play women. Women play themselves. Mainly because women ignore their intuition when it warns them that the man is on BS. They ignore the things that they see and the signs that they feel, without digging deeper to find out the truth.

When a man deflects when you do try to dig deeper, it's a clear sign that he's lying to you about something. However, many times you let whatever it is slide and you move forward, and this only enables him to continue to lie to you. You've heard me say it in other chapters, if you start to enable the liar, he knows all he needs to do is play dumb, give you some stupid excuse, and you'll go along with it. However, I truly believe women know when a man is lying and not keeping it real with them.

Stop fooling yourself. Be real with yourself about what you see and what you feel. If you're uncomfortable because you sense that he cannot give you a straight answer, listen to yourself, it's a warning. Especially when you confront him in a loving, calm manner. When you know you've done it the right way and he still can't come correct, walk away. Period.

You must show him that you're not going to entertain the lies. Even if he tries to guilt you into thinking, you're the one tripping. He feels like since you don't have any proof, you won't catch him. However, your gut is your proof. Again, I'm not talking about just jumping to conclusions, or simply going off hearsay. That's different. I'm not talking about that. I'm talking about when you tune into your inner voice and it tells you exactly what's going on. Trust it.

Lastly, don't get caught up in wondering and dwelling on why he lied. Again, lying is what people in general do to get a desired outcome. The quicker you understand that, the quicker you can bounce back from the lies people will tell you, including the lies that some men tell. Remember, the lies have nothing to do with you. Move forward and navigate through the bull and push past it.

Conclusion

*A*s I stated at the beginning of the book and in every chapter throughout, all men aren't liars. A man is not always lying to you. All men aren't dogs. All men aren't distrustful or looking for what they can get out of you. The purpose of this book was not to man bash or to make you jump to conclusions in every dating situation. The purpose was to shine a light on the reasoning behind why some men choose to lie in certain situations. I wanted you to be able to recognize what's going on in some of the common dating scenarios so that you're able to better protect yourself from being hurt.

I honestly hate the fact that I even had to write a book like this. I despise the fact that the great guys out here are being over-shadowed by the no-good men in the dating sphere. However, I am always going to keep it real, so better for me to address it than act like nothing's going on and good people aren't being affected.

With that said, I want to take a moment to remind you that there are a lot of good men still out here. A lot of great men. I say that sincerely. I'm not making that statement to blow smoke or to make you feel good. I'm speaking the truth. I'm sharing with you the fact that great men do really exist. I need you to embrace that fact so you can be open to receive yours. You can't receive what you don't believe. Open yourself up to that possibility.

Dating doesn't have to be as difficult as it may have been for you in the past or currently is. It should now be a lot easier going forward. You should now understand how to better navigate through the "no good for you men." Once you do, an amazing relationship is within reach. Always be willing to learn, grow, and cultivate the proper attitude and openness to experience greater success in your dating life and relationships.

Don't walk through life thinking that all your struggles are the result of the wrong men and not you. Doing this, gives men all the power. You're saying it's on them. That until they decide to act right, until they decide to not lie, until they decide to treat you the way you deserve, you just can't win. Thinking you'll never get the relationship you want. None of that is true. It's up to you to decide to love yourself no matter what.

Decide not to tolerate and entertain foolishness from men, especially men who don't belong in your life. When you start to do that, the wrong men will fall away, and the pathways will become clearer for the good picks to come your way.

Again, as I said in the very beginning of this book, my goal with this book is to help eliminate the damage caused by the lies some men tell women. I want to help break the negative cycles. I feel that if I give you the proper information, clarity, and honesty, I can help change the trajectory of your life because these types of situations can lead to so many problems. I don't want that to be your reality.

I hope you feel stronger and more confident from reading the information I shared. I hope you feel more secure and informed about navigating through the dating waters now. I hope you feel more empowered and positive about now knowing how to handle lying men and some common dating scenarios.

I hope you've gained some clarity and understanding on the dynamics of the lie's men tell when dating and in relationships that will help you be more successful in your own experiences. Dating and relationships are going to pose some obstacles that cause us to stumble or face some hard challenges. We might find ourselves in positions we never thought we would be in. But that's fine because the more you learn and understand how to handle these things, the more you avoid the damage that occurs from being caught up in the wrong situations.

No matter what, if you're going to engage in the dating sphere with men, I wanted you to understand what's going on, so you can see things more clearly and not get yourself caught up in any mess.

My last point and it may be the most important one of all. You need to spend time getting yourself prepared for the right relationship. If you've been wrapped up in any of the scenarios I covered in this book, you're not ready to entertain any kind of relationship until you embrace healing first. Going from one situationship to another doesn't help.

Instead, spend some time alone to grow and deal with the underlying issues that have caused you to entertain men who aren't right for you.

Before you'll be ready to meet the man, God has for you, I need you to embrace healing, cultivate your career, find your purpose. I don't want you to be so focused on men that you forget to take care of you. Focus on improving yourself personally and building your relationship with God. Once you do, you'll be truly ready to receive the great man you're destined to find true love with. I will go into this in more detail in my upcoming title, *Finding Love After Heartbreak, Volume I.*

A healthy relationship with yourself and God is ultimately the best repellent against the unloving habits of lying men.

Take your power back.

Love yourself first.

Author Disclaimer

The stories, characters, and scenarios used as examples throughout the book are based off real situations but have been fictionalized to protect the identities of my clients.

Any names or likeness to actual persons, either living or dead, is strictly coincidental. This book is designed to provide information and motivation to readers. Neither the publisher nor author shall be liable for any physical, psychological, emotional, financial, or commercial damages, including, but not limited to, special, incidental, consequential or other damages.

Every person is different and the advice and strategies contained herein may not be suitable for your situation. Our views and rights are the same: You are responsible for your own choices, actions, and results.

About The Author

Stephan Labossiere is *the* "Relationship Guy." An authority on real love, real talk, real relationships. The brand *Stephan Speaks* is synonymous with happier relationships and healthier people around the globe. For more than a decade, Stephan has committed himself to breaking down relationship barriers, pushing past common facades, and exposing the truth. It is his understanding of REAL relationships that has empowered millions of people, clients and readers alike, to create their best lives by being able to experience and sustain greater love.

Seen, heard, and chronicled in national and international media outlets including; the *Tom Joyner Morning Show, The Examiner, ABC*, GQ, and *Huffington Post Live*. The certified life & relationship coach, speaker, and award winning, bestselling author is the voice that the world tunes into for answers to their difficult relationship woes. From understanding the opposite sex, to navigating the paths and avoiding the pitfalls of relationships and self-growth, Stephan's relationship advice and insight helps countless men and women overcome the situations hindering them from achieving an authentically amazing life.

Stephan is highly sought-after because he is able to dispel the myths of relationship breakdowns and obstacles–platonic, romantic, and otherwise—with fervor and finesse. His signature style, relatability, and passion make international audiences sit up and pay attention.

"My message is simple: life and relationships require truth. The willingness to speak truth and the bravery to acknowledge truth is paramount."

Are you listening?

Enough said.

135

Coming Soon by
Stephan Speaks

www.FindingLoveAfterHeartbreak.com

Popular Books by
Stephan Speaks

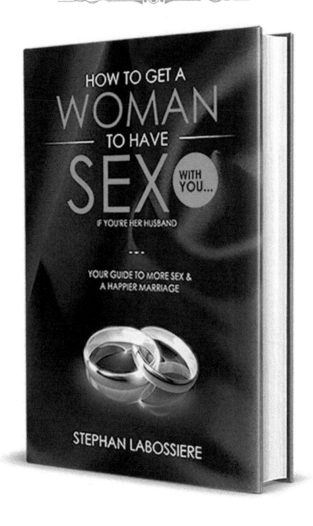

www.GetAManToCherishYou.com

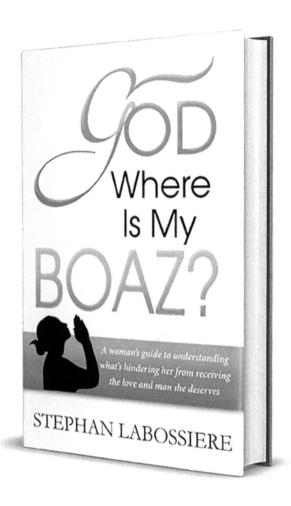

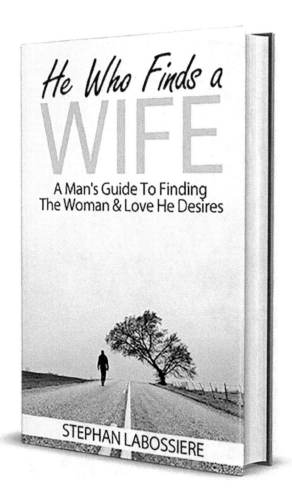

www.HeWhoFinds.com

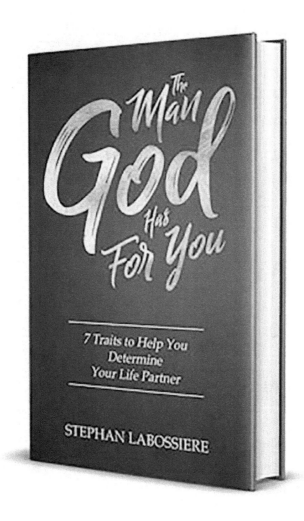

www.TheManGodHasForMe.com

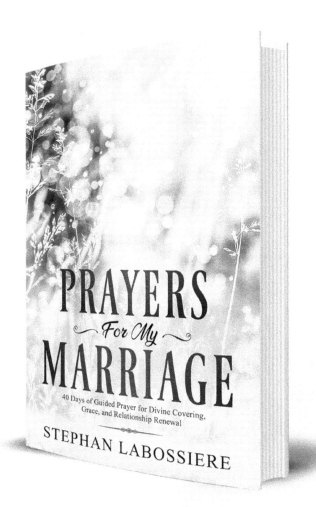

www.PrayersForMyMarriageBook.com

What Clients & Readers are saying about

Stephan Speaks!

INSIGHT & HONESTY

Stephan Labossiere has a rare blend of compassion, insight and honesty. He understands relationships, and is a supportive partner and guide on your journey to creating the love and life you want.

–Lisa Marie Bobby

HE'S FUN & LOVING

You hear people saying you must love yourself first, so you can attract the love of your life. This is what I wanted, and for me I did not quite know what this meant until I worked with Stephan. His work is fun, he is very loving, and you get results fast, because he sees very clearly what is going on. I truly recommend signing up for his coaching!

–Dominique, *Paris, France*

A JOY TO WORK WITH

As someone who has studied the role of men and women in relationships in our society for many years, it has been a joy to get to know and work with Stephan. His knowledge and candid from the heart writings and speaking on the topic of relationships are a breath of fresh air and sure to take you and your relationships to a more authentic and loving way of being.

–Tom Preston

More relationship resources can be found at
www.StephanSpeaks.com/shop/

You can also follow me on
Twitter & Instagram: **@StephanSpeaks**
or find me on Facebook under
"Stephan Speaks Relationships"

CPSIA information can be obtained
at www.ICGtesting.com
Printed in the USA
JSHW022151240520
5858JS00014B/14